SECOND EDITION **1**
Workbook

Herbert Puchta · Peter Lewis-Jones · Günter Gerngross · Helen Kidd

CAMBRIDGE
UNIVERSITY PRESS

Contents

Friends

1 **Read and match. Colour the circles.**

1 ⬤ I'm Whisper.　2 ◯ I'm Flash.　3 ◯ I'm Thunder.　4 ◯ I'm Misty.

a ◯

b ◯

c ◯

d ⬤

1 Look and match.

a seven
b three
c ten
d eight
e nine
f one
g four
h five
i two
j six

2 Write the number words.

a t e h r e   three

b e o n   o _____

c x i s   s _____

d o w t   t _____

e n e v s e   s _____

f n n i e   n _____

g h t e i g   e _____

h u o r f   f _____

i n e t   t _____

j v e f i   f _____

3 Look. Then write about you.

1 What's your name?

I'm _____ .

2 How old are you?

I'm _____ .

I'm Sam.
I'm six.

1 🛡 🎧01 **Can you remember? Listen and write.**

E̶ E G T Q X

---

1 Colour the words.

purple orange
yellow red
green blue

2 Write your name. Then draw a picture of you.

Hi, I'm _____.

1 🎧 02 **Who says it? Listen and tick ☑.**

2 **Match the Super Friends with the powers.**

1

2

3

4

a

b

c

d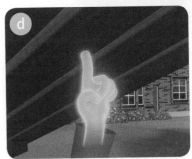

1 Write and circle.

1 I can write the names of ten numbers. Yes / No

one _____ _____ _____ _____ _____

_____ _____ _____ _____ _____

2 What colour is the balloon?
   The balloon is green / red.

3 What colour is the bag?
   The bag is blue / purple.

2 Write the letters.

In the alphabet …

1 what's after 'B'? _C_

2 what's after 'E'? ___

3 what's before 'K'? ___

4 what's after 'M'? ___

5 what's before 'R'? ___

6 what's before 'T'? ___

  3 Read. Then draw and write.

Hi! I'm Alex. I'm six. _____

My bag is yellow. Look! _____

1 At school

1 Look and match.

1 desk
2 bag
3 pencil
4 notebook
5 rubber
6 book
7 pen
8 paper
9 ruler
10 pencil case

2 Look and colour.

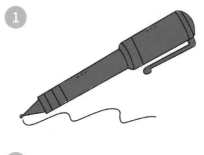

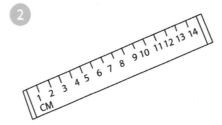

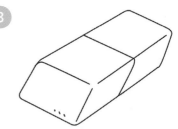

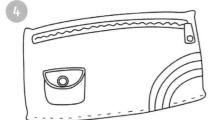

Key

1 Look and write.

is   isn't   it   ~~this~~

1 What's _this_ ?

2 Is _____ a pencil?

3 No, it _____ .

Is it a ruler?

4 Yes, it _____ .

2 Read and tick ☑.

1 What's this? Is it a desk?

☐ Yes, it is.   ☑ No, it isn't.

2 What's this? Is it a pencil case?

☐ Yes, it is.   ☐ No, it isn't.

3 What's this? Is it a pencil?

☐ Yes, it is.   ☐ No, it isn't.

4 What's this? Is it a rubber?

☐ Yes, it is.   ☐ No, it isn't.

Can you remember? Listen and write.

What's this? What's this? Please tell me, what's this?

(1) Is it a _pen_____? (2) Is it a _____?

Come on, take a look.

(3) It's a _____ … (4) It's a _____ …

2 **Look and write.**

1 Is it a bag?

_No, it isn't._____

2 Is it a book?

Yes,_____

3 Is it a pen?

_____

4 Is it a ruler?

_____

5 Is it a rubber?

_____

6 Is it a pencil case?

_____

1 **Write the words.**

get   Open   ~~Sit~~   Write

(1) __Sit_____ at your desk, please.

(2) Now _____ a pen.

(3) _____ your book, please.

(4) _____ one to ten.

2 **Look and number the pictures.**

1 Open your book, please.

2 Write one to ten.

3 Now get a pen.

4 Sit at your desk, please.

5 Close your bag, please.

6 Pass me a pen, please.

a   4

b

c

d

e

f

1   Who says it? Listen and tick ☑.

2 Look and tick ☑ or cross ☒.

In the story, Flash's friends have …

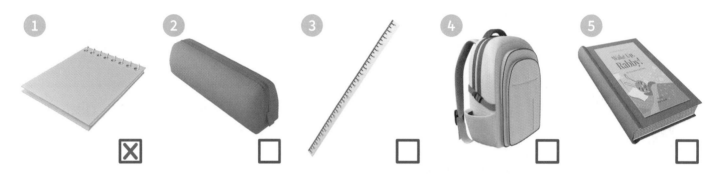

1 ☒ 2 ☐ 3 ☐ 4 ☐ 5 ☐

3 Who says it? Match.

1 Flash, come back!

2 Pass me the box, please.

3 Here's your book.

4 Watch out!

a   b   c   d

Who says what? Write numbers.

1 Here's your book. 2 Watch out! 3 I'm sorry.

2 05 **Write and match. Listen and say.**

1 A c_a_t

2 A f__t r__t

3 A bl__ck h__t

4 A bl__ck b__g

1 Look and read. Tick ✓ or cross ✗.

1 This is a book.

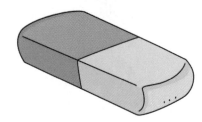

2 This is a pencil case. ☒

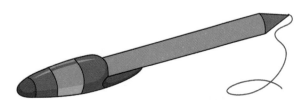

3 This is a pencil. ☐

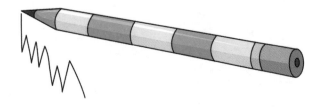

4 This is a pen. ☐

5 This is a ruler. ☐

6 This is a notebook. ☐

1 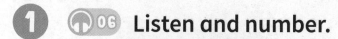 **Listen and number.**

1

2 **Draw and write about your pencil case.**

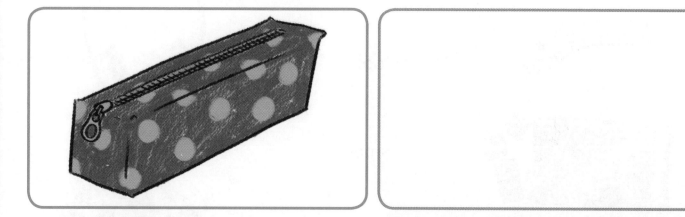

This is my pencil case.

It's blue and pink.

Think and learn

Senses

1 Look and write.

| look | listen | ~~smell~~ | taste | touch |

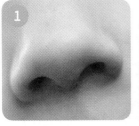   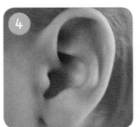 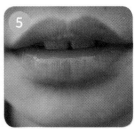

smell _____ _____ _____ _____

2 Look and match.

1

a taste

b look

2

3

c smell

4

d touch

5

e listen

3 **Look and write.** Look   Listen   Taste

_____ to this song!

_____ at this shell!

_____ this ice cream!

4 **Choose and draw.**

look   listen   ~~smell~~   taste   touch

smell

_____

1   Make a pencil holder.

You need

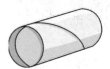
toilet roll tube

scissors

cardboard

glue

magazines

1
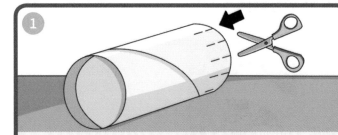
Cut flaps at the bottom of the toilet roll tube.

2
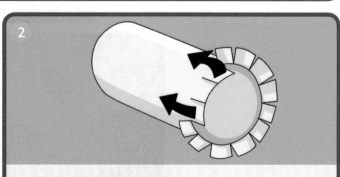
Fold the flaps out.

3
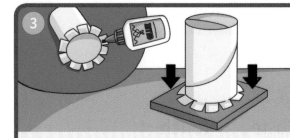
Glue the flaps on the piece of cardboard.

4

Cut out pictures from magazines.

5

Glue the pictures on the tube.

6

Now you have a pencil holder.

1 Write and circle.

1 I can write the names of five classroom objects. Yes / No

pen _____ _____ _____ _____ _____

2 What's this? Is it a rubber?

Yes, it _____. / No, it _____.

3 What's this? Is it a notebook?

Yes, it _____. / No, it _____.

2 Look and write.

BIG QUESTION How do we learn?

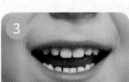 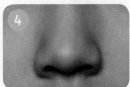 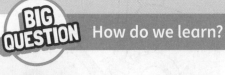 

look   l_____   t_____   s_____   t_____

3 Read. Then draw and write.

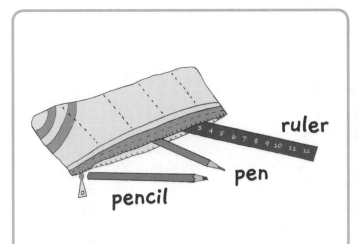

ruler

pen

pencil

This is my pencil case. _____

It's yellow and green. _____

2 Let's play

1 Look and number.

1 train   **2** plane   **3** monster   **4** kite   **5** bike

6 ball   **7** doll   **8** car   **9** computer game   **10** go-kart

2 Join the dots. What is it? Write.

It's a _____.

1 Draw lines and write.

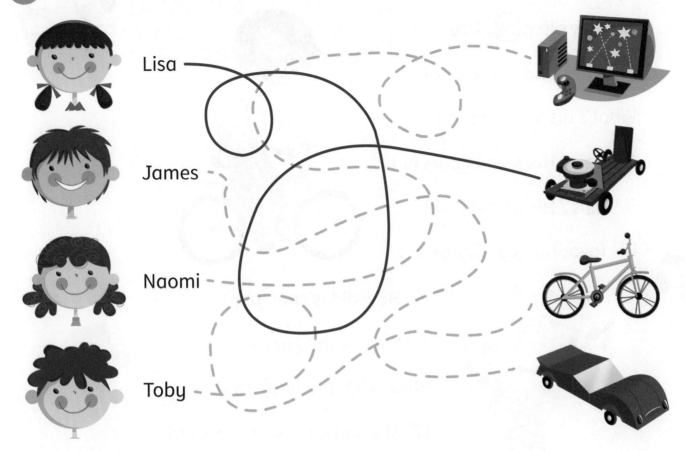

1 Her name's Lisa. Her favourite toy's her __go-kart__.

2 His name's James. His favourite toy's his _____.

3 Her name's Naomi. Her favourite toy's her _____.

4 His name's Toby. His favourite toy's his _____.

2 Read and match.

1 What's his name?   a He's ten.

2 How old is he?   b She's eight.

3 What's his favourite toy? c His name's Ben.

4 What's her name?   d Her name's Kate.

5 How old is she?   e Her favourite toy's her plane.

6 What's her favourite toy? f His favourite toy's his train.

1   **Can you remember? Listen and circle.**

(1) How old is **he** / **his**?

(2) What's **he** / **his** name?

What's his favourite toy?

(3) **He's** / **His** seven years old.

(4) **He's** / **His** name's Mike.

His favourite toy's his bike …

(5) How old is **she** / **her**?

(6) What's **she** / **her** name?

What's her favourite toy?

(7) **She's** / **Her** seven years old.

(8) **She's** / **Her** name's Jane.

Her favourite toy's her plane.

2 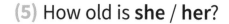 **Draw and write about you.**

My name's

_____.

I'm _____ years old.

My favourite toy's my _____.

1 **Look, read and tick ☑.**

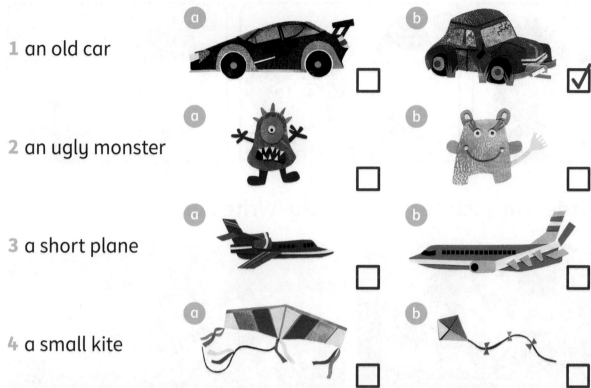

1 an old car
   a ☐   b ☑

2 an ugly monster
   a ☐   b ☐

3 a short plane
   a ☐   b ☐

4 a small kite
   a ☐   b ☐

2 **Write the words in the correct order.**

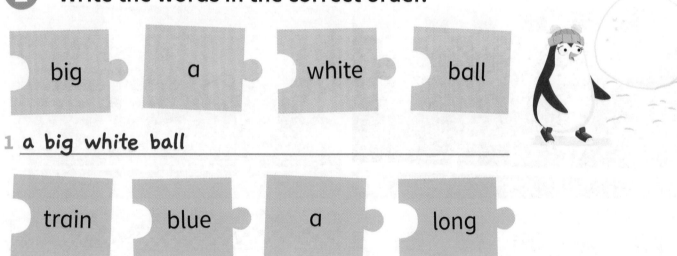

| big | a | white | ball |

1 <u>a big white ball</u>

| train | blue | a | long |

2 _____

| bike | a | new | red |

3 _____

1 🎧 **08** **Who says it? Listen and tick** ✔.

2 🛡 **Order the pictures in the story. Write numbers.**

1   **Who says it? Tick ☑ the correct picture.**

That isn't fair!

2 🎧09 **Write *e* or *a*. Listen and say.**

1 c **a** t

2 p___n

3 p___ncil

4 b___g

5 d___sk

6 t___n

7 bl___ck

8 Fl___sh

Fair play; phonics focus 27

1 🎧 **10** **Listen and colour.**

2 🛡 **Look and write.**

Her favourite things

Her favourite **number is four**_____.

Her favourite _____

_____.

Her favourite _____

_____.

1 Read, number and colour.

1 a big yellow doll

2 a long blue train

3 an ugly green monster

4 a new black bike

5 a short red train

6 an old purple bike

7 a beautiful black monster

8 a small pink doll

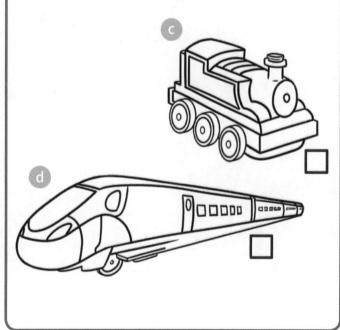

1 **Look and write.**

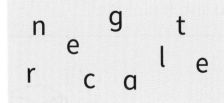

1 <u>r e c t a n g l e</u> 2 _____

3 _____ 4 _____ 5 _____

2 **Look and match.**

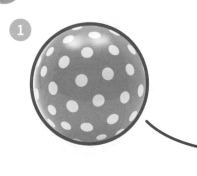

1

a triangle

2

b kite

c rectangle

d circle

e square

3

4

5

3 🛡️ **Which shapes are in the toys? Look and tick ☑ or cross ☒.**

1

a triangle ☑

b kite ☒

c circle ☑

2

a square ☐

b triangle ☐

c kite ☐

3

a rectangle ☐

b square ☐

c circle ☐

4 🛡️ **Read and look at Activity 3. Write the names of the toys.**

1 A triangle and two circles. _bike_

2 A square, a rectangle and two circles. _____

3 A kite and four triangles. _____

5 🛡️ **Choose, write and draw.**

| rectangle   square   circle   ~~triangle~~   kite |

triangle

1 Make a paper kite.

You need

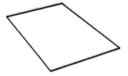
paper

pens

stapler

hole punch

string

1
Colour the paper.

2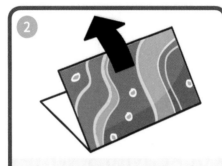
Fold the paper in half.

3
Bend one side of the paper.

4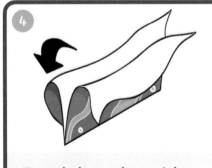
Bend the other side.

5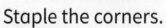
Staple the corners.

6
Make a hole.

7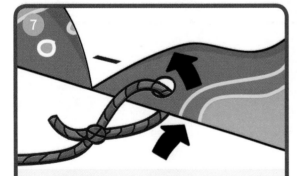
Put the string through the hole and tie a knot.

8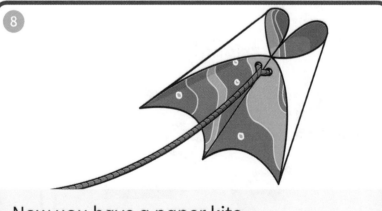
Now you have a paper kite.

1 Write and circle.

1 I can write the names of five toys.   Yes / No

train _____ _____ _____ _____

2 What's his name? He's / His name's Tom.

3 How old is he? He's / His seven.

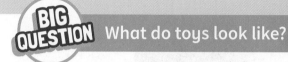

2 Write the words. Then draw.

BIG QUESTION What do toys look like?

1 s<u>quare</u>   2 r<u>e</u>   3 c<u>i</u>   4 t<u>r</u>   5 k<u>i</u>

3 Read. Then draw and write.

rectangle

circle

My favourite toy is my car.

It's an old red car.

1 Look and write.

cat	dog	donkey
duck	elephant	frog
~~spider~~	lizard	rat

```
1 s
  p
  i
3 d
  e
5       6   7
  r
8
9
4
```

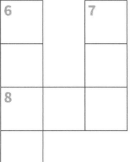

2 Write and draw.

My favourite animal's a _____. Look!

1 Look and tick ☑.

1 The elephant is under the car.	☑ Yes	☐ No
2 The cat is on the car.	☐ Yes	☐ No
3 The frog is in the car.	☐ Yes	☐ No
4 The spider is on the car.	☐ Yes	☐ No
5 The duck is under the car.	☐ Yes	☐ No

2 Look and write.

on   in   under

(1) The frog's _____ my bag. (2) It's _____ my chair.

(3) It's not _____ my hat. It isn't there.

1   **Can you remember? Listen and write.**

(1) The frog's __on_____ a bag

And that's not good.

(2) Put the _____ in the pond,

(3) Yes, the pond _____ the wood …

(4) The duck's _____ the car

And that's not good.

(5) Put the _____ on the pond,

(6) Yes, the pond _____ the wood …

2 **Read, draw and colour.**

1 a rat in the pond   3 a dog in the bag   5 a cat on the bike

2 a duck on the pond   4 a lizard under the bike

1 Read and write the numbers.

1

2

a I like ducks. ☑ 4

b I don't like frogs. ☐

3

c I like frogs. ☐

d I like lizards. ☐

4

e I don't like lizards. ☐

f I don't like ducks. ☐

5

6

2 Write the words.

I like   I don't like

I like frogs. What about you?

1 _____ frogs, too.

2 _____ big frogs.

1 🎧 12 Who says it? Listen and tick ☑.

① ☐ ☐

② ☐ ☐

③ ☐ ☐

2 🛡 Look and match. Draw lines.

① He's amazing!

② Touch him, Misty.

③ Look, he's under the table.

a

b

c

3 🛡 Order the pictures in the story. Write numbers.

a ☐

b ☐

c 1

d ☐

1   **Which boy is brave? Tick ☑ the correct picture.**

2 🎧 13 **Read, draw and colour. Listen and say.**

1 a **b**ig pan

2 **s**ix pens

3 a **p**ink desk

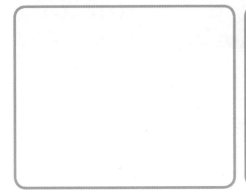

4 a bla**ck** rat

5 a red **c**at

6 ten ba**gs**

1 Read and write the numbers.

 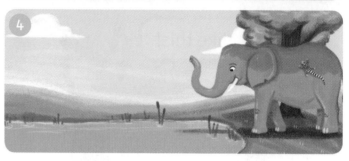

a The elephant is under the tree. The lizard is on the elephant.   [4]

b The elephant is in the pond. The spider is on the elephant.   ☐

c The elephant is under the tree. The spider is on the elephant.   ☐

d The elephant is in the pond. The lizard is on the tree.   ☐

2 Look and find three differences. Circle and write.

Picture 1	Picture 2
ten ducks	nine ducks

1 🎧 14 **Listen and draw lines.**

2 🛡 **Look at the picture in Activity 1 and write.**

1 The donkey is <u>under the tree</u>   .

2 The duck is _____.

3 The dog is _____.

4 The cat is _____.

5 The spider is _____.

Think and learn

Nature

1 **Look and write.** | air food ~~shelter~~ water

It needs …

shelter _____ _____ _____

2 **What does it need? Tick ☑ the objects.**

 ☑

 ☐

 ☐

 ☐

 ☐

 ☐

3 What is it? Write the numbers.

food
____   ____
____

water
1   ____
____

shelter
____   ____
____

4 Draw and write about an animal.

Cat

It eats cat food.

It drinks water.

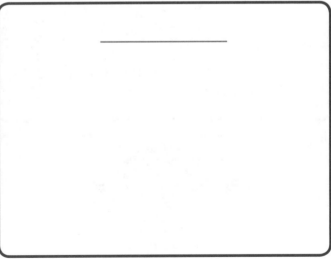

____

1 **Make an animal mask.**

You need

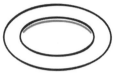 

paper plate   pencil   scissors   pens   hole punch   elastic or string

1

Put the paper plate on your face. A grown-up marks where your eyes are.

2
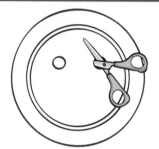
A grown-up cuts out the eyes.

3

Colour the mask and draw a nose and a mouth.

4

A grown-up makes two holes at the sides.

5

Tie elastic or string to the two sides.

6

Now you have an animal mask.

Write and circle.

1 I can write the names of five animals.   Yes / No

frog _____ _____ _____ _____ _____

2 The dog's in / on the bag.

3 The cat's on / under the desk.

---

2 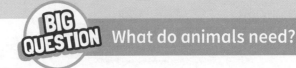 **Read and tick ☑ or cross ☒.**

BIG QUESTION What do animals need?

Animals need ...

1 food ☑   **2** books ☐   **3** shelter ☐   **4** air ☐   **5** water ☐

About me! **3** **Read. Then draw and write.**

I like lizards.

I don't like dogs.

_____

_____

1 Look and number.

1 pizza   2 chicken   3 apples   4 cheese

5 cake   6 sausages   7 bananas   8 carrots

2 Circle the food words.

steakcarrotfishrainbananascatpizzaapplebagpeas

1 Look and circle.

1 I **'ve got** / **haven't got** a sandwich.

2 I **'ve got** / **haven't got** a sausage.

3 I **'ve got** / **haven't got** an apple.

4 I **'ve got** / **haven't got** pizza.

5 I **'ve got** / **haven't got** a cake.

6 I **'ve got** / **haven't got** a banana.

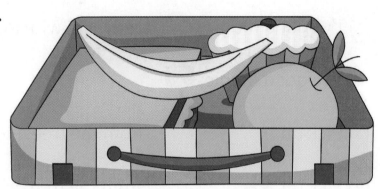

2 Read and match.

1. I've got a banana and an apple. I haven't got a carrot.

2. I've got a banana and a carrot. I haven't got an apple.

3. I've got two carrots. I haven't got a banana and I haven't got an apple.

4. I've got two apples. I haven't got a carrot and I haven't got a banana.

3 Look and write. | 've   got   haven't |

(1) I've _____ a carrot.

(2) I _____ got a carrot.

Look what I can do ...

(3) Now I _____ got a carrot!

1 🛡️ 🎧 15 **Can you remember? Listen and write.**

(1) I've got a magic 🌳 <u>tree</u> with lots of things to eat.

(2) I've got a magic 🌳 _____. Let's go and get a treat.

(3) Pick an 🍦 _____ from the tree. Pick an 🍊 _____ from the tree.

(4) Pick an 🍎 _____ from the tree. It's there for you and me.

(5) I've got a magic 🌳 _____ with lots of things to take.

(6) I've got a magic 🌳 _____. Let's go and get a 🍰 _____ ...

2 🛡️ **Which foods grow on trees? Draw.**

1 Who says what? Look and circle.

1 Penny, I'm hungry. Have we got any fish?

Paul / Penny

2 No, we haven't. We haven't got any fish.

Paul / Penny

3 Yes, we have! Yes, we've got a fish.

Paul / Penny

2 Look at the picture and answer the questions.

1 Have we got any pizzas?

Yes, we have.

2 Have we got any peas?

No, we haven't.

3 Have we got any steaks?

_____

4 Have we got any orange juice?

_____

3 Look and write questions.

1  Have we got any apples?

2 _____

3 _____

1 🎧 16 **Who says it? Listen and tick ☑.**

2 🛡 **Look and match. Draw lines.**

We've got pizza.

1 2

Pizza, please.

3 **Look and write.** What have you got? Here you are.

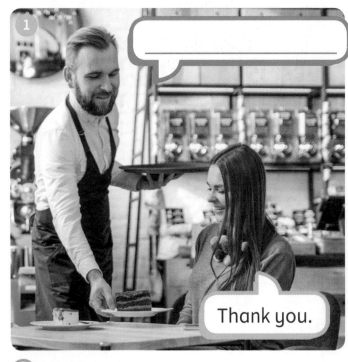

Thank you.

I've got a cheese sandwich.

1 **Read and match. Tick ☑ the correct picture.**

What is he doing? It's unfair!

2 🎧 17 **Listen and colour. Point and say.**

Key a = black   e = red   o = orange   i = pink

  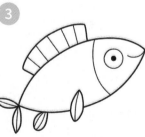 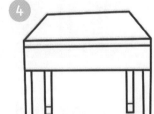

   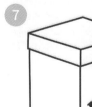  

1 Look at the numbers. Look at the letters. Write the words.

1 **13**   t h i r t e e n

2 **17**   s _ _ _ _ _ _ _ _ _ _

3 **15**   f _ _ _ _ _ _ _

4 **12**   t _ _ _ _ _

5 **20**   t _ _ _ _ _

6 **18**   e _ _ _ _ _ _ _ _

2 Look and write.

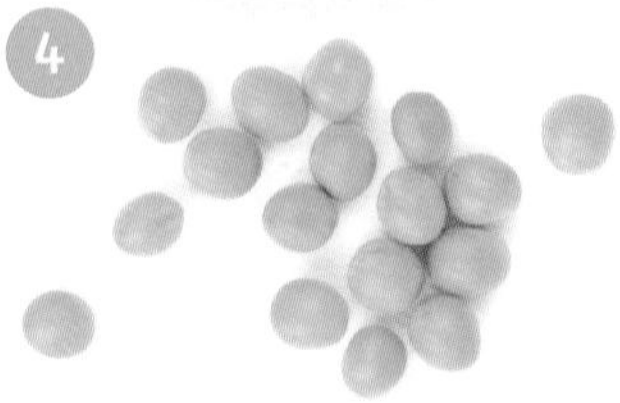

1 twelve
   bananas

2 _____

3 _____

4 _____

1 **Listen and tick ☑.**

1 What's in the cake?

a  ☐

b ☐

c ☐

2 Where's the food?

a ☐

b ☐

c ☐

2 🛡 **Read and match. Write numbers.**

1 I like pizza and peas. I don't like apples or milk.

2 I like pizza and carrots. I don't like bananas or milk.

3 I like sausages and carrots. I don't like bananas or orange juice.

4 I like sausages and peas. I don't like apples or milk.

a  ☐

b  ☐

c  ☐

d  1

Food

1 **Look and write.** fruit vegetables plant tree ~~soil~~

soil _____ _____ _____ _____

2 **Where does the food grow? Look and match. Then write _fruit_ or _vegetable_ under the pictures.**

vegetable _____ _____

in the soil   on a plant   on a tree

_____ _____ _____

3 **G** Order the pictures. Write numbers.

a

Now the carrot is **big**_____.

b

I eat the carrot. It's my _____!

c 1

The carrot is _____.

d

The carrot is _____.

4 Look at Activity 3. Write the words to complete the sentences.

> in a shop   ~~big~~   in the soil   dinner

5 **G** Find out about the food in your house. Draw and write.

> in the soil   on a plant   on a tree   fruit   vegetable

Food	🍎			
Fruit or vegetable?	fruit			
Where does it grow?	on a tree			

1   Make a place mat.

You need

| card | magazines | scissors | glue | pens |

1

Cut out pictures of food from magazines.

2

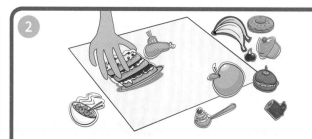

Think about where to put the pictures on the card.

3

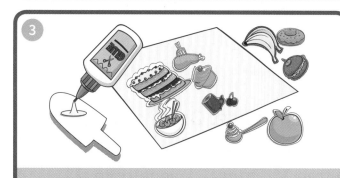

Glue the pictures on the card.

4

Draw a border.

5

Write your name.

6

Now you have a place mat.

1 Write and circle.

1 I can write the names of five foods.   Yes / No

sausage   _____   _____

_____   _____

2 Have they got any pizzas?

Yes, they _____ . / No, they _____ .

2 Look, read and circle.

BIG QUESTION Where does food come from?

It grows …

1

in the soil / on a tree

2

on a tree / in the soil

3

in the soil / on a plant

About me! 3 Read. Then draw and write.

My lunch

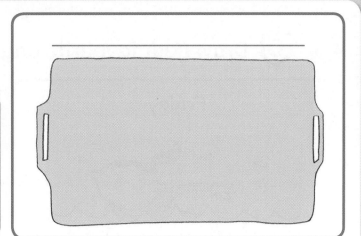

I've got a cheese sandwich
and a banana.

5 Free time

1 Write the days of the week.

1. aFiyrd **Friday**

2. ndSayu _ _ _ _ _ _

3. dnesWayed _ _ _ _ _ _ _ _ _

4. Sdyaatur _ _ _ _ _ _ _ _

5. ayueTsd _ _ _ _ _ _ _

6. shTdyaur _ _ _ _ _ _ _ _

7. yMoadn _ _ _ _ _ _

2 Draw your favourite day and write.

Friday

My favourite day is Friday.

1 Look, read and match. Write numbers.

On Saturdays, …

a ▢2 b ▢ c ▢ d ▢

1 I play with my toys.
2 I play computer games.

3 I ride my horse.
4 I go swimming.

2 Write the words in the correct order.

1 I / Sundays / ride / on / horse / my   <u>I ride my horse on Sundays</u> .

2 Fridays / I / piano / play / on / the   _____ .

3 Saturdays / go / I / on / swimming   _____ .

4 play / Tuesdays / football / on / I   _____ .

5 on / I / my / Wednesdays / ride / bike   _____ .

3 Write the words.

     like   go   play

(1) I _____ swimming
on Mondays, swimming in the sea.

(2) I _____ football on Tuesdays.
Come and play with me! …

(3) But on Saturdays and Sundays,
I _____ being with you.

I (watch TV) on (Sundays). 59

1   **Can you remember? Listen and draw lines.**

1 Monday

2 Tuesday

3 Wednesday

4 Friday

5 Saturday

6 Sunday

2 **What do you do? Write and draw a picture.**

On Mondays, I _____
_____.

On Tuesdays, I _____
_____.

On Sundays, I _____
_____.

1 Read and circle the correct words.

1 Do you watch TV at the weekend? No, I **do** / **don't**.

2 Do you ride your bike with Paul? Yes, I **do** / **don't**.

2 Read and match. Then write answers.

1 Do you play football at the weekend? <u>Yes, I do.</u>

2 Do you sing songs at the weekend? <u>No, I don't.</u>

3 Do you play computer games at the weekend? _____

4 Do you ride a horse at the weekend? _____

5 Do you play the piano at the weekend? _____

6 Do you go swimming at the weekend? _____

3 Write and tick ✓.

	Yes, I do.	No, I don't.
1 Do you <u>ride</u> your bike at the weekend?	☐	☐
2 Do you _____ fishing at the weekend?	☐	☐
3 Do you _____ TV at the weekend?	☐	☐

1 🎧 20 **Who says it? Listen and tick ✓.**

2 🛡 **Look and write the numbers.**

1 Are you OK, Rabbit?

3 Watch out!

5 Rabbit, we're lost.

2 I don't know.

4 Here you are, Rabbit.

a — Yippee!

3

b — ___

Come with me.

c — ___

Where's the lake?

d — ___

e — ___

1   **Look and write.** We're lost. Come with me.

2 🎧 21 **Write the words. Listen and say the sentences.**

rat ~~lunch~~ milk pens rubber dog

Mum and her **lunch** . Ken and his _____ . Jill and her _____ .

Polly and her _____ . Sam and his _____ . Gus and his _____ .

1 Read and draw lines to make sentences.

1 On Mondays, I play with

2 On Tuesdays, I ride

3 On Wednesdays, I play

4 On Thursdays, I go

5 On Fridays, I ride my

6 On Saturdays, I play the

7 On Sundays, I watch

a computer games.

b horse.

c piano.

d my friends.

e TV.

f swimming.

g my bike.

2 Look at Activity 1. Write the days.

a

b

c

d

Tuesday _____   _____   _____

e

f

g

_____   _____   _____

1 🎧 22 **What do they do? Listen and tick ☑.**

1 On Mondays, James …

2 On Wednesdays, Emma …

3 On Fridays, Charles …

4 On Saturdays, Hannah …

2 🛡 **Look at Activity 1 and write the names.**

1 __James_____ plays football on Mondays.

2 _____ watches TV on Fridays.

3 _____ plays with her friends on Wednesdays.

4 _____ rides her horse on Saturdays.

Think and learn
Activities

1 **Look and write.**

> go climbing　　go running　　go skiing
> go sledging　　go surfing　　~~go swimming~~

go swimming

2 **Where can we do it? Look and write the numbers.**

1 go climbing

2 go running

3 go skiing

4 go sledging

5 go surfing

6 go swimming

1

3 Read, look and match.

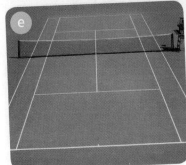

1 We ride a horse here.

2 We play football here.

3 We go fishing here.

4 We go running here.

5 We go climbing here.

6 We play tennis here.

4 What do they do? Look and write.

1 I _go swimming_.

2 I _____.

3 I _____.

4 I _____.

1 Make a guitar.

You need

tissue box

paint and brushes

elastic bands of different sizes

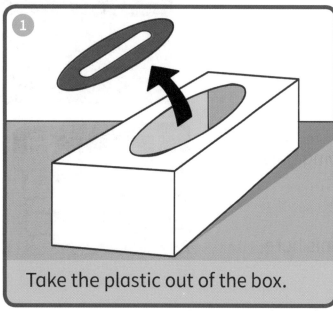

1 Take the plastic out of the box.

2 Paint the box.

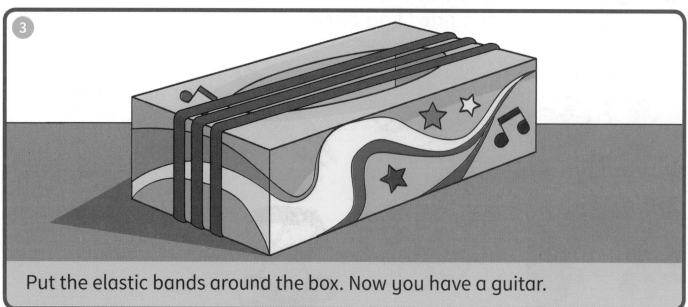

3 Put the elastic bands around the box. Now you have a guitar.

1 What do I know? Write and circle.

1 I can write the names of the days of the week.   Yes / No

Monday _____   _____   _____   _____

_____   _____   _____

2 Do you watch TV at the weekend?   Yes, I _____. / No, I _____.

2 Look and read. Tick ✓ or cross ✗.

 BIG QUESTION   Which activities do we do?

 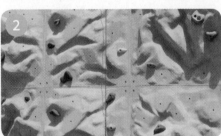 

We go skiing here. ☐   We go surfing here. ☐   We go running here. ☐

3 About me! Read. Then draw and write.

 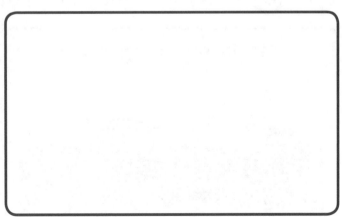

On Saturdays, I play football. _____

_____

6 The old house

1 **Write the words.**

| bathroom | cellar | stairs | kitchen |
| living room | ~~hall~~ | bedroom | dining room |

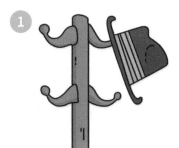 1

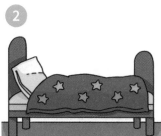 2

 3

 4

hall _____   _____   _____   _____

 5

 6

 7

 8

_____   _____   _____   _____

2 **Choose a room. Write and draw.**

Me in my living room

_____

1 Look and circle.

1

(**There's**) / **There are** a frog on the piano.

2

There's / **There are** a butterfly on the flower.

3

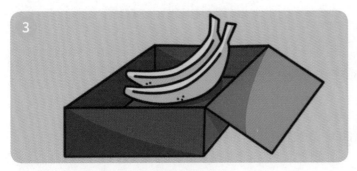

There's / **There are** bananas in the lunchbox.

4

There's / **There are** a lizard on the log.

5

There's / **There are** apples on the tree.

6

There's / **There are** a football on the TV.

2 Write the words.

There are   There's

(1) _____ a fish in the hall …

(2) _____ three fish in the kitchen.

1 🛡️ 🎧 23 **Can you remember? Listen and write.**

We live in different homes, you and me. Me and you. You and me …

(1) You live in a ___flat___ and I live in a _____!

(2) Some people live in houses, some people live in _____,

(3) Some people live in flats, or in _____ under the stars …

Some homes are very old, some homes are new,

Some homes are very small, some have got beautiful views …

2 🛡️ **Read and circle. Draw two homes.**

Some homes are **old** / **new**.

Some homes are **big** / **small**.

1 **Complete the questions.**

| Are | ~~Is~~ | How many | Is there | Are there |

(1) __Is_____ there a park?   No, there isn't.

(2) _____ a school?   Yes, there is.

(3) _____ there any trees?   No, there aren't.

(4) _____ any houses?   Yes, there are.

(5) _____ are there?   There are two.

2 **Look and write *Yes* or *No*. Then circle.**

1 Is there a butterfly on a flower?   __Yes___, there (is)/ **isn't**.

2 Are there any bananas on the tree?   _____, there **are** / **aren't**.

3 Is there a frog on the log?   _____, there **is** / **isn't**.

4 Are there any bikes on the grass?   _____, there **are** / **aren't**.

1 🎧 24 **Who says it? Listen and tick ☑.**

2 **Look and write.**

The stairs to the cellar!

Big spiders!

1 How many are there?

e_____t

2 How many are there?

t_____e

3 **What does Misty say? Look and write the numbers.**

1 You can come in

2  house

3 me

Misty: There's the old ☐. Let's go in.

Misty: Let me go in. Wait for ☐ here.

Misty: There's no problem. ☐.

1   **Who looks after a friend? Tick ☑ the correct picture.**

2 🎧 25 **Write the words. Listen and say.**

hat   hall   ~~house~~   hot   happy   hairy

1 a small _house_

2 a _____ spider

3 a big _____

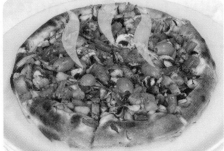

4 a _____ girl

5 a _____ pizza

6 a blue _____

1 Look and read. Write *yes* or *no*.

1 The house has got a cellar.   <u>yes</u>

2 There are two boys and two girls.   <u>no</u>

3 There's a chair in the bathroom.   _____

4 There are three dolls in the bedroom.   _____

5 The dog has got a ball.   _____

6 There's a guitar in the kitchen.   _____

2 Look at Activity 1. Read and match.

1 They play football here.   a in the kitchen

2 They have dinner here.   b in the bedroom

3 They play the piano here.   c in the garden

4 There's a desk here.   d in the living room

1 🎧26 Listen and colour.

2 Look at the picture in Activity 1 and complete the sentences.

1 There 's one_____ bike.

2 There _____ cats.

3 There _____ football.

4 There _____ trees.

Think and learn

Homes

1 **Look and write.**

| cave house   house boat   ~~tree house~~   yurt |

tree house

2 **Read and write the numbers.**

My house is in water.

My house is in a tree.

My house is round.

a yurt ☐   **b** house boat 1   **c** tree house ☐

3  **Read, match and circle.**

1 Which home is it?

2 How many rooms are there?

3 What has it got?

4 What hasn't it got?

a There are **three** / **five** rooms.

b It's got a **kitchen** / **hall**.

c It hasn't got a **cellar** / **living room**.

d It's a (**tree house**)/ **house boat**.

4 **Read. Write a poem puzzle. Decorate.**

Which home is it?

Has it got __stairs__ ?
__No__ !

Is it __round__ ? __Yes__ !

What is it? It's a
__yurt__ !

Which home is it?

Has it got _____?
_____!

Is it _____? _____!

What is it? It's a
_____!

1 🛡 Make a pop-up house.

You need

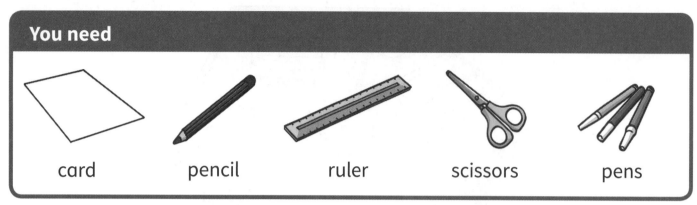

card   pencil   ruler   scissors   pens

1
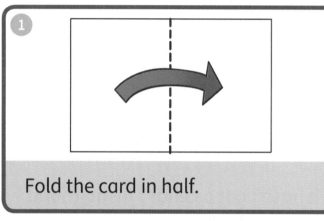
Fold the card in half.

2
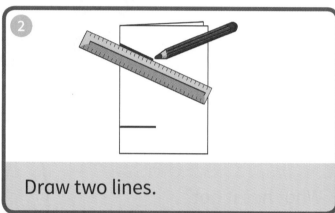
Draw two lines.

3
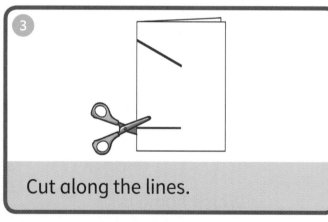
Cut along the lines.

4
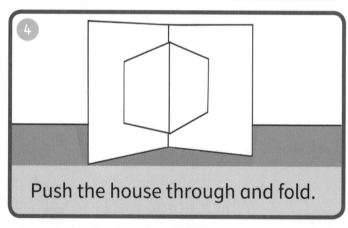
Push the house through and fold.

5

Open the card. Colour the house.

6

Now you have a pop-up house.

1 **Write and circle.**

1 I can write the names of five rooms in a house.   Yes / No

__bedroom__   _____   _____   _____   _____

2 Are there any stairs in your house?

Yes, there _____. / No, there _____.

BIG QUESTION How are houses different?

2 **Write the words.**

c__ave__   h__ouse__   h_____ b_____   y_____   t_____ h_____

3 **Read. Then draw and write.**

stairs   my bedroom   bedroom   bathroom   bedroom

__My home has got three__
__bedrooms and a bathroom.__   _____
_____

7 Get dressed

1 Find the clothes. Look → and ↓. Circle.

h	u	s	o	c	k	s	c	j	j	x
T	s	h	i	r	t	g	y	a	e	j
b	a	s	e	b	a	l	l	c	a	p
s	h	d	s	k	i	r	t	k	n	e
h	c	w	v	e	b	r	k	e	s	a
o	s	h	o	r	t	s	u	t	z	v
e	s	w	e	a	t	e	r	f	m	o
s	t	r	o	u	s	e	r	s	l	k

2 Look and write the words from Activity 1.

1   2   3   4   5

socks _____ _____ _____ _____ _____

6   7   8   9   10

_____ _____ _____ _____ _____

1 Read and write the numbers.

a I like these shorts. ☑3️⃣

b I like this T-shirt. ☐

c I don't like this T-shirt. ☐

d I don't like these shorts. ☐

2 Circle the words.

1 Do you like **this** / (**these**) jeans?

2 Do you like **this** / **these** baseball cap?

3 Do you like **this** / **these** skirt?

4 Do you like **this** / **these** socks?

5 Do you like this sweater?
No, I **do** / **don't**.

6 Do you like these trousers?
Yes, I **do** / **don't**.

3 Write the words.

do	~~this~~	don't	these

(1) Do you like **this** _____ hat?

(2) Yes, I _____.

(3) Do you like _____ shoes?

(4) No, I _____.

1   **Can you remember? Listen and write.**

(1) Do you like this <u>purple</u> <u>sweater</u> ?

(2) Do you like this big,  _____ _____?

Yes, I like your hat and sweater. You look good like that …

(3) Do you like these _____ _____?

(4) Do you like this _____?

Yes, I like your cap and trousers. You look good like that …

2 **Read, draw and colour.**

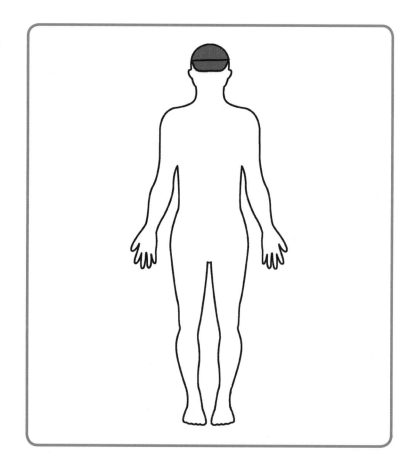

· a purple baseball cap

· yellow socks

· green shoes

· an orange sweater

· blue trousers

· a red jacket

1 **Read and look. Point to Sam.**

Look, that's Sam!

Is he wearing a blue cap? _____

No, he isn't.

Is he wearing a red cap?

Yes, he is. Sam's wearing a red cap.

Wave to him!

Sam _____

2 **Read and write the names under the pictures in Activity 1.**

Kim is wearing a yellow sweater, blue shorts and a yellow baseball cap.
Sam is wearing a white T-shirt, orange shorts and a red baseball cap.
Tim is wearing a green jacket, blue jeans and a blue baseball cap.
Jo is wearing a purple T-shirt and black jeans.

3 **Look at the pictures in Activity 1. Read and circle *yes* or *no*.**

1 Is Tim wearing blue jeans? (yes)/ no

2 Is Jo wearing a baseball cap? yes / no

3 Are Kim and Sam wearing shorts? yes / no

4 Are Sam and Jo wearing jackets? yes / no

1 🎧 28 **Who says it? Listen and tick ☑.**

2 🛡 **Write the names. Who's wearing … ?**

1 these shoes?

2 this cap?

3 this skirt?

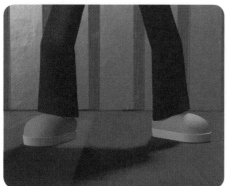

_____

_____

_____

3 🛡 **Who says it? Match.**

1 Look! Gary's wearing my cap.

3 That's my cap!

2 No problem.

4 Maybe Gary has got the same cap.

a

b

c

1   **Look and write.** It's OK. I'm very sorry.

2 29 **Write the letters. Listen and say.**

sw   st   sk   st   sp   sch   st   sn

1 **st** op

2 ___ider

3 ___eak

4 ___eater

5 ___irt

6 ___airs

7 ___ool

8 ___ake

1 🎧 30 **Listen and colour.**

2 **Read and write the numbers.**

a She's wearing a blue T-shirt and blue shorts. She's playing football. ☐

b He's wearing a white T-shirt. He's putting socks in a box. ☐

3 **Write about pictures one and two in Activity 2.**

1 He's **wearing a yellow baseball cap**. He's _____.

2 She's _____. She's _____.

1 **Look at the pictures and read the questions. Write one-word answers.**

1 What's the boy doing?

He's _____.

2 Where are the boy and the girl?

In the _____.

3 What's the boy doing?

He's playing computer _____.

4 What's the girl doing?

She's watching _____.

5 How many cats are there?

There are _____.

6 Where are the cats?

Under the _____.

Patterns

1 **Look and write.**

plain   stripes   ~~spots~~   zigzags   flowers

spots _____   _____   _____   _____   _____

2 **Read and match.**

1 a skirt with spots

2 a sweater with zigzags

3 plain jeans

4 shoes with flowers

5 socks with stripes

6 a plain jacket

3 Design some trousers. Then write.

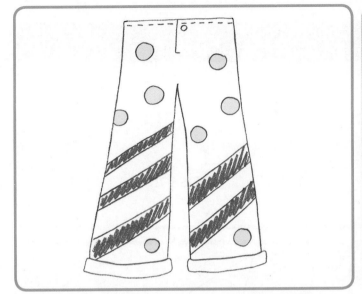

They're white trousers with red stripes and yellow spots.

They're _____ trousers with _____ _____ and _____ _____.

4 Find out about your clothes. Complete the chart.

My clothes	
with spots	6 socks
with stripes	2 T-shirts
with zigzags	sweater
with flowers	shorts
plain	3 skirts

My clothes	
with spots	_____
with stripes	_____
with zigzags	_____
with flowers	_____
plain	_____

1 Make a party hat.

You need

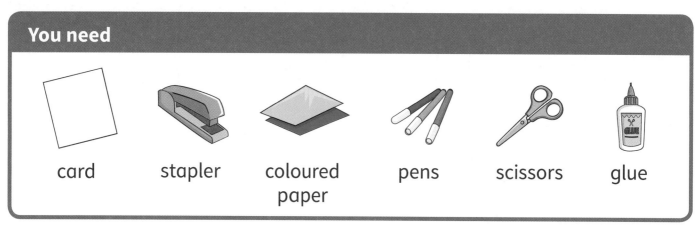

card   stapler   coloured paper   pens   scissors   glue

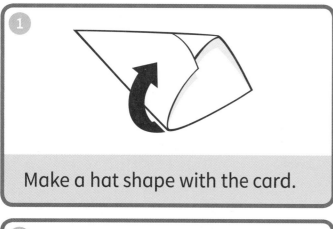

1 Make a hat shape with the card.

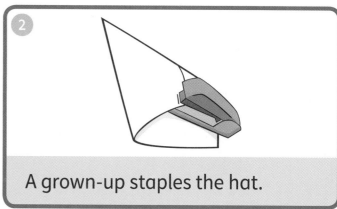

2 A grown-up staples the hat.

3 Cut out shapes and stick them on the hat.

4 Draw a pattern on the hat.

5 Now you have a party hat.

1 **Write and circle.**

1 I can write five names for clothes.   Yes / No

trousers   _____   _____

_____   _____

2 Do you like this sweater with stripes?

Yes, I _____ . / No, I _____ .

2 🛡 **Draw patterns and write.**

BIG QUESTION How do clothes look different?

1 s_tripes_   2 f_____   3 p_____   4 s_____   5 z_____

3 🛡 **Read. Then draw and write.**

I'm wearing a T-shirt with red and white stripes, blue jeans and orange shoes.

_____
_____
_____

1 Make parts of the body. Write the letters. | s a d g e o |

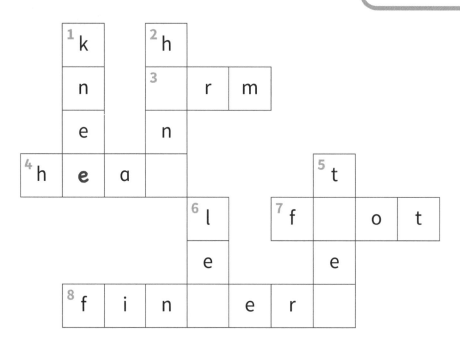

¹k		²h				
n		³	r	m		
e		n				
⁴h	e	a			⁵t	
		⁶l		⁷f	o	t
		e		e		
⁸f	i	n		e	r	

2 Look and write.

  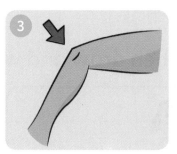 

1 _leg_

2 _____

3 _____

4 _____

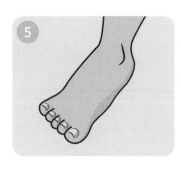  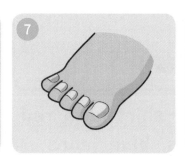 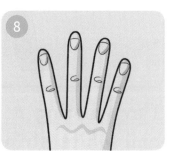

5 _____

6 _____

7 _____

8 _____

1 Read and write the numbers.

1 I can stand on one leg.

2 I can skip.

3 I can touch my toes.

4 I can't stand on one leg.

5 I can't skip.

6 I can't touch my toes.

2 What can Penny do? Write *can* or *can't*.

(1) I __can__ stand on one leg …

(2) I _____ skip.

(3) I _____ swim.

(4) I _____ sing.

(5) But I _____ fly.

1 🛡 🎧 31 **Can you remember? Listen and write.**

(1) I can take my  _____ and put it on my head.

(2) I can take my _____ and put it on my leg.

I can put my tongue out and I can touch my nose.

(3) I can take my right _____.

(4) And touch all of my _____.

(5) I can cross my _____.

(6) And I can cross my _____.

But now I'm stuck. Oh dear! Can you help me, please?

2 🛡 **What can you do? Draw and write.**

I can **touch my toes** _____. I can _____.

1 Look, write and tick ☑.

1 <u>Can he</u> play the piano?

☐ Yes, he can.   ☑ No, he can't.

2 _____ ride a bike?

☐ Yes, she can.   ☐ No, she can't.

3 _____ swim?

☐ Yes, he can.   ☐ No, he can't.

4 _____ ride a horse?

☐ Yes, she can.   ☐ No, she can't.

2 Look and write the answer for you.

1 Can you cook?   2 Can you draw?   3 Can you dance?

<u>Yes</u>, I <u>can</u>.   _____, I _____.   _____, I _____.

1 🎧 **32** Who says it? Listen and tick ☑.

 1 ☐ ☐

 2 ☐ ☐

 3 ☐ ☐

2 Write the words.

done   Here   ~~problem~~   try

1

2 No **problem** .

3 _____ you are.

4

5

6 Let me _____ something.

8 Well _____, Misty.

7

3 🛡 Look at the pictures in Activity 2. Write the numbers.

a Thank you, Misty. 7

b Batteries! We haven't got batteries. ☐

c We've got a problem. ☐

d Thank you. ☐

1   **Which picture shows good teamwork? Tick ☑.**

2 🎧 33 **Write and match. Listen and say.**

1 _**g**_ rey

2 fro___

3 computer ___ame

4 ___arden

5 fin___ers

6 le___

7 do___

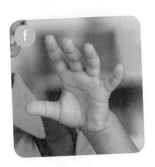

1  Read and tick ✓ or cross ☒.

Hi, I'm Ben. I can touch my toes, but I can't skip. I can play the piano and I can play football, but I can't play tennis. I can ride a bike, but I can't ride a horse.

Hi, I'm Anna. I can skip, but I can't touch my toes. I can play the piano and I can play tennis, but I can't play football. I can ride a bike and I can ride a horse.

Hi, I'm Tom. I can touch my toes and I can skip. I can play tennis and I can play football, but I can't play the piano. I can ride a bike, but I can't ride a horse.

	touch toes	skip	play the piano	play football	play tennis	ride a bike	ride a horse
Ben	✓						
Anna							
Tom							

2 Look at Activity 1. Write.

1 Ben, can you ride a bike?   Yes, I can.

2 Ben, can you skip?   No, I can't.

3 Anna, can you touch your toes?   _____

4 Anna, can you play tennis?   _____

5 Tom, can you ride a bike?   _____

6 Tom, can you play the piano?   _____

1 🎧 34 **Read the questions. Listen and write a name or a number.**

1 What's the girl's name? <u>Karen</u>

2 How old is she? <u>   </u>

3 What's the dog's name? <u>   </u>

4 How many lizards has the girl got? <u>   </u>

5 What's the horse's name? <u>   </u>

Think and learn

Movements

1 **Look and write.**

forwards   backwards   stretch
sideways   ~~step~~   jump

step _____

2 🛡 **Read and draw lines. Write.**

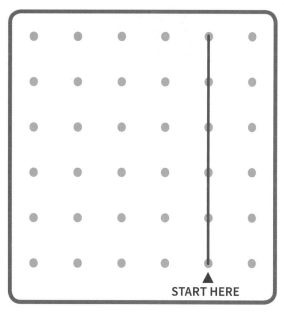

START HERE

1 Go five steps 👣 forwards ↑ .

2 Go three steps 👣 sideways to the left ← .

3 Go five steps 👣 backwards ↓ .

4 Go three steps 👣 sideways to the right → .

Look. What shape is it? It's a _____ .

3 🛡 **Read and write the numbers.**

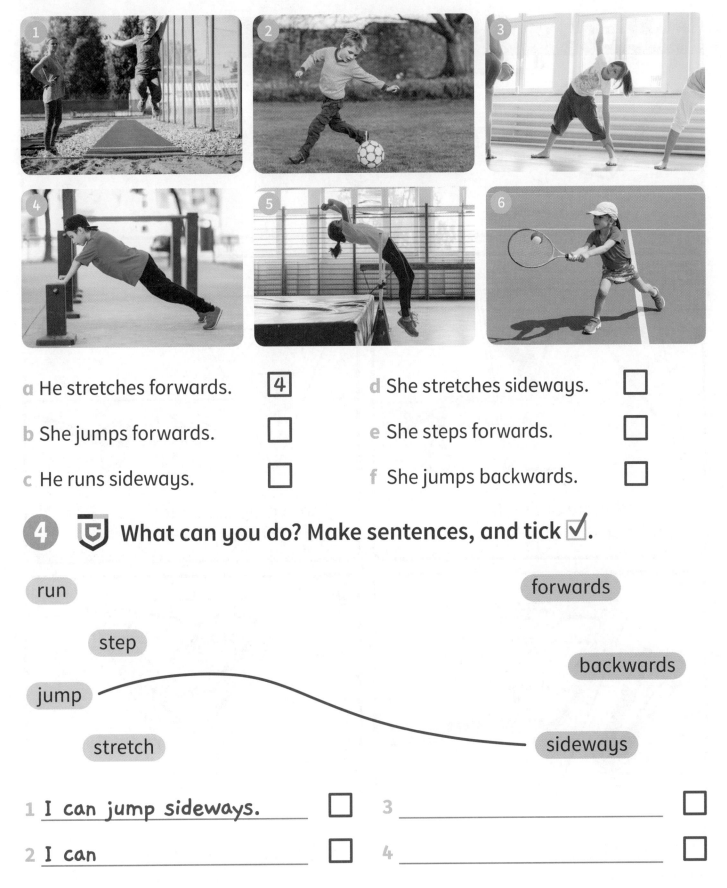

a He stretches forwards. 4

b She jumps forwards. ☐

c He runs sideways. ☐

d She stretches sideways. ☐

e She steps forwards. ☐

f She jumps backwards. ☐

4 🛡 **What can you do? Make sentences, and tick ☑.**

run   forwards

step   backwards

jump

stretch   sideways

1 I can jump sideways. ☐   3 _____ ☐

2 I can _____ ☐   4 _____ ☐

1 🛡 Make a robot mask.

You need

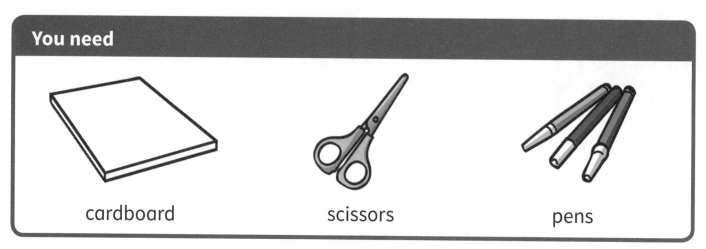

cardboard   scissors   pens

①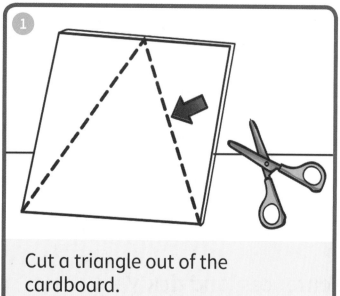

Cut a triangle out of the cardboard.

②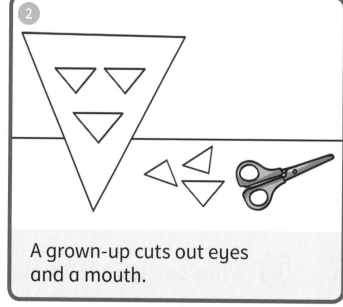

A grown-up cuts out eyes and a mouth.

③

Colour the mask.

④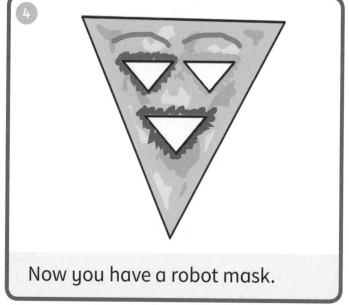

Now you have a robot mask.

1 Write and circle.

1 I can write the names of five parts of the body. Yes / No

foot _____ _____ _____

_____ _____

2 Can you cross your legs?

Yes, I _____ . / No, I _____ .

2 Write the movement words.

BIG QUESTION How can we move?

1 r f o
r w s a d

forwards

2 k c
s a w d r
a b

b_____

3 e i s d
a y s w

s_____

4 p j u
m

j_____

5 s t
e p
e

s_____

3 About me!   Read. Then draw and write.

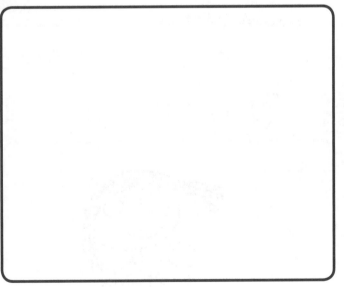

I can **run backwards, but** I can _____

I can't touch my toes . _____ .

9 At the beach

1 Write the words.

1

look for **shells**

2

take a _____

3

catch a _____

4

paint a _____

5

listen to _____

6

eat _____

7

read a _____

8

make a _____

9

play the _____

2 Read. Then write and draw.

I'm eating ice cream.

_____

1 Write the words.

make   look   read   ~~listen~~   catch   take

1 Let's **listen** to music. Good idea.

2 Let's _____ a fish. I'm not sure.

3 Let's _____ some photos. Sorry, I don't want to.

4 Let's _____ a book. Good idea.

5 Let's _____ for shells. Sorry, I don't want to.

6 Let's _____ a sandcastle. Good idea.

2 Look and match with Activity 1. Write the numbers.

a  4

b □

c □

d  □

e  □

f  □

1 🛡 🎧 35 **Can you remember? Listen and write.**

(1) Let's go to the mountains and _climb a tree_____ .

(2) Let's _____, you and me.

The holidays, the holidays, the holidays are near.

The holidays, the holidays, it's the end of the year!

(3) Let's go to the beach and _____ .

(4) Let's _____, you and me.

The holidays, the holidays …

(5) No! Let's stay at home and _____ .

(6) Let's _____, just you and me.

The holidays, the holidays …

2 🛡 **Write two more sentences for the song. Draw pictures.**

Let's _____

_____ .

Let's _____

_____ .

1 Write the words.

It's	They're	~~Where are~~	Where's

(1) __Where are__ my sunglasses? (2) _____ on my head!
(3) _____ my cap? (4) _____ on my head!

2 Look and match.

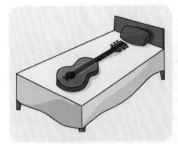   

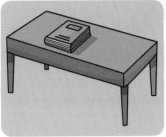   

1 Where's the guitar?

2 Where are the shells?

3 Where's the fish?

4 Where are the birds?

5 Where's the book?

6 Where's the shell?

7 Where's the photo?

8 Where's the ice cream?

a It's in the book.

b It's in the sea.

c They're on the sandcastle.

d It's on his T-shirt.

e It's on the bed.

f It's on the sandcastle.

g It's on the desk.

h They're in the box.

1 🎧 36 **Who says it? Listen and tick ☑.**

1 ☐ ☐

2 ☐ ☐

3 ☐ ☐

2 **Write the words.**

end   hill   ~~race~~   top

1
A _race_?

2
Bye. See you at the
_____ of the _____!

3
This is the _____
of the race.

3 🛡 **Look and write the numbers.**

1 Let's go together.

2 What a good idea!

3 Let me try.

a ☐
Thanks, Thunder.

b ☐
Now you can race
to the top, Flash!
No. ____. That's
more fun!

c ☐
Yes!

1 Who shows modesty? Look and tick ✓ the correct picture.

1 My picture's fantastic!

2 I really like your picture.

2 🎧 37 Write *ee* or *ea* and match. Listen and say.

1 s**ee**___
2 r**ea**___d
3 thr_____
4 ch_____se
5 _____t
6 b_____ch
7 p_____s
8 ice cr_____m

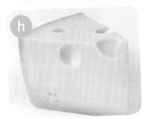

1 **Read. Choose a word from the box. Write the correct word next to numbers 1–6.**

It's a lovely day at the beach. The **(1)** <u>sun</u> is hot and the
(2) _____ is cool. There are lots of children. One boy's making
a **(3)** _____. It's very big. There's a little girl. She's wearing a
(4) _____ on her head and she's eating an **(5)** _____.
There's a man. He's playing a **(6)** _____.

What a lovely day at the beach!

shell ☐   sun ☑   hat ☐   sea ☐

guitar ☐   castle ☐   sandcastle ☐   ice cream ☐

1 🎧 38 Listen and number.

1 Jim

2 Pip

3 Sue

4 Liz

5 Bob

6 Mia

7 Tom

8 Kay

2 🛡 Look at the picture in Activity 1. Write the names.

a

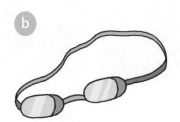
b

c

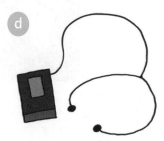
d

Liz _____

e

f

g

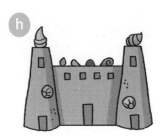
h

_____ _____ _____ _____

Think and learn

Landscapes

1 **Look and write.**

mountains   countryside   beach
~~city~~   theme park   campsite   lake

city _____

_____   _____   _____

2 **Read. Then look at the pictures in Activity 1. Write the numbers.**

a We can make a sandcastle here. ☐ 7   e We can ride on fun things here. ☐

b We can climb up here. ☐   f We can see lots of trees here. ☐

c We can sleep in a tent here. ☐   g We can go to shops here. ☐

d We can go on a boat here. ☐

3 Read and match.

1 I'm in a city. I can take photos here.

2 I'm in the mountains. I can go skiing here.

3 I'm in the countryside. I can see birds here.

4 I'm at a campsite. I can sleep here.

5 I'm at the beach. I can go surfing here.

4 Choose, write and draw.

the mountains ~~the countryside~~
the beach the city

I like **the countryside**.
I can **climb a tree** here.

I like _____.
I can _____ here.

1   Make a holiday scrapbook.

You need

 white paper

 coloured paper

 hole punch

 string

 pens

 photos

1
Put the white paper together.

2
Put the coloured paper on top.

3
Make two holes in the paper.

4
Put the string through the holes. Tie a knot.

5
Draw a picture on the cover.

6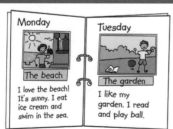
Monday

Tuesday

The beach
I love the beach! It's sunny. I eat ice cream and swim in the sea.

The garden
I like my garden. I read and play ball.

Draw pictures or stick in photos. Write sentences.

7
Now you have a holiday scrapbook.

1 Write and circle.

What do I know?

1 I can write four things to do at the beach.   Yes / No

look for shells _____   _____

_____   _____

2 Let's listen to music. ☑   Good idea. / Sorry, I don't want to.

3 Let's play the guitar. ☒   Good idea. / Sorry, I don't want to.

2 Draw places and write.

BIG QUESTION Where can we go on holiday?

1 c ity _____   2 m _____   3 l _____

3 Read. Then draw and write.

About me!

My holiday

I look for shells. _____

I eat ice cream. _____

_____

Friends

nine   two   ~~one~~   seven   four
five   three   eight   ten   six

1 one _____

2 _____

3 _____

4 _____

5 _____

6 _____

7 _____

8 _____

9 _____

10 _____

1 At school

notebook   ~~bag~~   ruler   desk   book
pencil case   pencil   rubber   pen   paper

bag

2 Let's play

car　　doll　　kite　　~~ball~~　　computer game
plane　　go-kart　　bike　　train　　monster

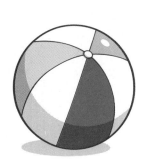

ball

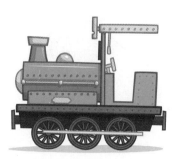

rat   duck   frog   donkey   ~~cat~~
elephant   spider   dog   lizard

cat

_____   _____   _____

_____   _____   _____

_____   _____   _____

4 Lunchtime

chicken   peas   carrots   pizza   cheese sandwich
~~apples~~   bananas   cake   steak   fish   sausages

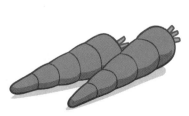

apples

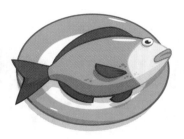

nineteen ~~eleven~~ twelve eighteen fourteen
fifteen thirteen seventeen twenty sixteen

11 12 13

eleven _____ _____ _____

14 15 16 17

_____ _____ _____ _____

18 19 20

_____ _____ _____

5 Free time

Monday ~~Monday~~   Friday   Sunday   Tuesday   Wednesday   Saturday   Thursday

Monday

Tuesday

Wednesday

Thursday

Monday _____

Friday

Saturday

Sunday

_____

| dining room | living room | cellar | bedroom |
| kitchen | ~~bathroom~~ | hall | stairs |

bathroom

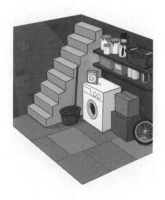

7 Get dressed

shorts   socks   jeans   ~~baseball cap~~   trousers
skirt   T-shirt   shoes   jacket   sweater

baseball cap

_____

_____

_____

_____

_____

_____

_____

_____

_____

8 The robot

leg   ~~arm~~   toes   head   fingers   hand   knee   foot

arm

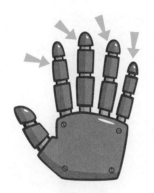

_____

_____

_____

_____

_____

_____

9 At the beach

paint a picture   ~~catch a fish~~   take a photo
listen to music   eat ice cream   play the guitar
read a book   look for shells   make a sandcastle

catch a fish

_____

_____

_____

_____

_____

_____

_____

_____